JULY 2023

FOSSILS

THIS EDITION
Editorial Management by Oriel Square
Produced for DK by WonderLab Group LLC
Jennifer Emmett, Erica Green, Kate Hale, *Founders*

Editors Grace Hill Smith, Libby Romero, Maya Myers, Michaela Weglinski;
Photography Editors Kelley Miller, Annette Kiesow, Nicole di Mella; **Managing Editor** Rachel Houghton;
Designers Project Design Company; **Researcher** Michelle Harris; **Copy Editor** Lori Merritt;
Indexer Connie Binder; **Proofreader** Larry Shea; **Reading Specialist** Dr. Jennifer Albro;
Curriculum Specialist Elaine Larson

Published in the United States by DK Publishing
1745 Broadway, 20th Floor, New York, NY 10019

Copyright © 2023 Dorling Kindersley Limited
DK, a Division of Penguin Random House LLC
23 24 25 26 10 9 8 7 6 5 4 3 2 1
001–334109–July/2023

A catalog record for this book
is available from the Library of Congress.
HC ISBN: 978-0-7440-7514-4
PB ISBN: 978-0-7440-7515-1

DK books are available at special discounts when purchased in bulk for sales promotions, premiums,
fundraising, or educational use. For details, contact: DK Publishing Special Markets,
1745 Broadway, 20th Floor, New York, NY 10019
SpecialSales@dk.com

Printed and bound in China

The publisher would like to thank the following for their kind permission to reproduce their images:
a=above; c=center; b=below; l=left; r=right; t=top; b/g=background
123RF.com: alexeykonovalenko 21cra, Galyna Andrushko 8-9, Camilo Maranchon 18-19; **Alamy Stock Photo:** Kevin Schafer 11tr;
David Clark Inc: 8crb; **Depositphotos Inc:** Pecold 18bl; **Dorling Kindersley:** Colin Keates / Natural History Museum 27cr,
Colin Keates / Natural History Museum, London 1cb, 12tl, 12tr, 12cla, 13t, 13c, 14bl, 14br, 22b, Gary Ombler, Oxford University
Museum of Natural History 3cb; **Dreamstime.com:** Linda Bucklin 23t, Pablo Caridad 28-29, Gluk54 4-5, Scott Jones 17b,
Likrista82 16tl, 16tr, Lucagal 29cl, W.scott Mcgill 21tl, Damian Pawlos 15tl, Patrick Poendl 13bl, Maksim Shchur 20tl, Siloto 15cra,
Taweesak Sriwannawit 26tr, Petr Svec 24-25; **Fotolia:** Elena Blokhina 26bl; **Getty Images:** gorodenkoff 10-11,
Mark Stevenson / Stocktrek Images 6-7; **Getty Images / iStock:** E+ / benedek 29tr, milehightraveler 19cr, OlgaPtashko 26-27;
Science Photo Library: Science Stock Photography 20br

Cover images: *Front:* **Getty Images / iStock:** Mik122; *Back:* **Dorling Kindersley:** Gary Ombler,
Oxford University Museum of Natural History cl

All other images © Dorling Kindersley
For more information see: www.dkimages.com

For the curious
www.dk.com

FOSSILS

Libby Romero

Contents

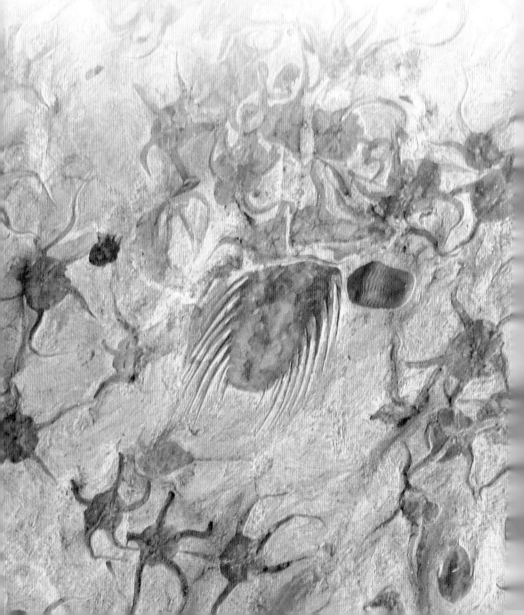

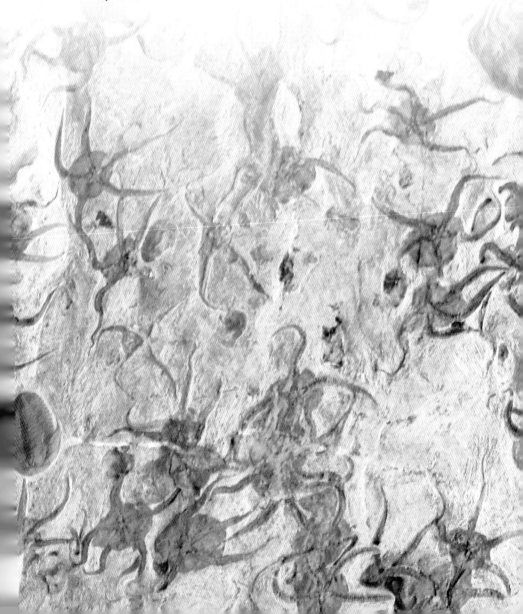

Introducing Fossils

About 80 million years ago, in the Gobi region of modern-day Mongolia, a *Velociraptor* moved stealthily across the arid land. The feathered dinosaur was about the size of a wolf. It sniffed the air in search of prey. It spotted a *Protoceratops*. A fight for all time was about to take place.

Velociraptor

The *Velociraptor* pounced. It pierced the *Protoceratops* in the neck with one of its sharp claws. But the plump herbivore fought back and managed to get on top. It chomped down on the *Velociraptor*'s right arm with its parrot-like beak. The carnivore's arm snapped.

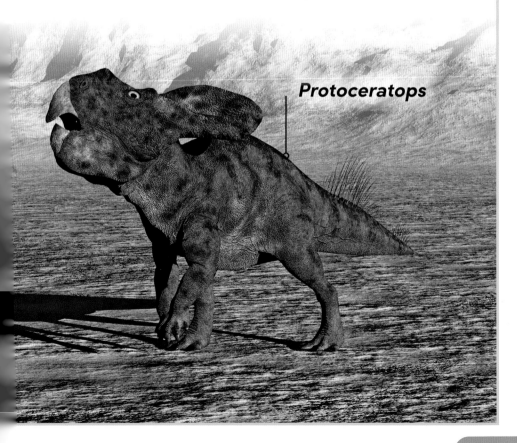

Protoceratops

Is this exactly what happened? Maybe, maybe not. But a mass of sand, possibly a collapsed dune, suddenly swept over the enemies—right in the middle of their fight.

Millions of years passed. In 1971, paleontologists discovered the remains of these dinosaurs, preserved mid-fight. It is one of the most amazing fossils ever found.

Important Find
The fossil of the fighting dinosaurs is considered a national treasure of Mongolia.

Fossils are evidence of past life. Sometimes, they are the preserved remains of ancient organisms. Other times, they are traces, or signs of life, that the organisms left behind. Some fossils are dramatic, like the fighting dinosaurs. Others may just look like rocks— unless you know what you're looking for.

Most fossils found today come from ancient plants or animals that lived in or near water. The sedimentary rocks that hold these fossils formed when layers of sediment built up in lakes, swamps, and oceans and hardened over time. The preserved remains are found on land now because Earth has changed. Land that was once covered by water might be found in deserts or mountains today.

Fossils Everywhere
Dinosaur fossils have been found on every continent, including Antarctica.

That's why paleontologists don't just study fossils. They scour the area where fossils are found, looking for clues about ancient plants and animals. The clues help them understand the history of life on Earth.

Types of Fossils

There are two main kinds of fossils: body fossils and trace fossils.

Body fossils show what an ancient organism looked like. These fossils formed when a living organism died and was quickly buried by mud, sand, or volcanic ash. Soft parts quickly decomposed. But the hard parts, like bones, remained.

Over time, minerals seeped into spaces in the hard parts. The minerals turned hard as stone. Layers of sediment piled up. Eventually, the land shifted or was worn away. This brought the fossils to the surface.

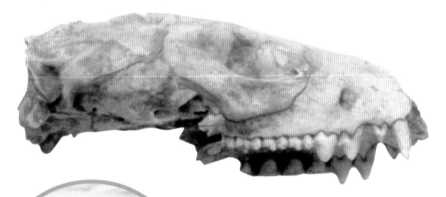

Body Fossils

Many body fossils are the preserved remains of animals, such as bones, teeth, and claws. But trees can make body fossils, too. Over time, the wood petrifies, or becomes as hard as stone.

Molds are another type of body fossil. A mold forms when an organism dissolves and leaves an imprint of its shape behind. Many fossil molds were formed by shells. Some molds show what shells were like on the outside. Others show what the shells were like on the inside. They formed after sediments filled the hollow shells.

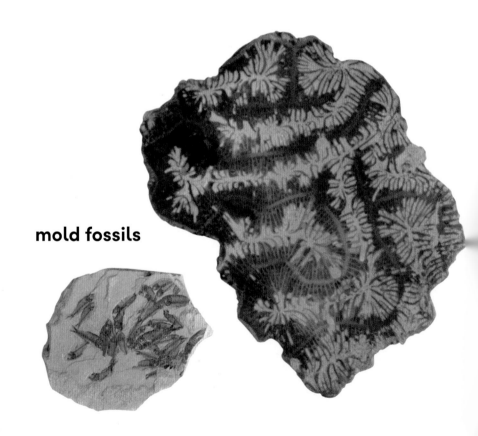

mold fossils

cast fossils

Sometimes, deposits of minerals filled the molds instead. The minerals hardened. They formed a cast in the shape of the organism. Casts are another type of body fossil.

Paleontologists often make artificial casts to recreate the skeletons of ancient organisms. Some displays in museums are artificial casts instead of the real thing.

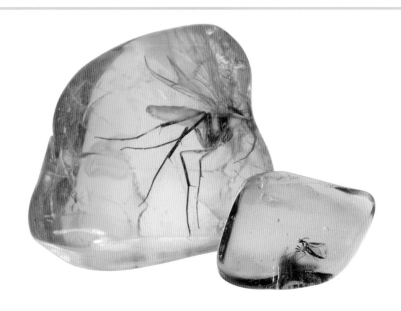

It is rare for an entire organism—soft parts and all—to be preserved as a fossil. But it does happen. One way is with amber. Ancient plants, animals, and even dinosaur feathers got stuck in sticky tree resin. It hardened and turned to amber, or fossilized resin, trapping them inside.

Entire organisms have also been preserved in tar and ice. Millions of fossils—including massive ground sloths, mastodons, and saber-toothed cats—have been excavated from the La Brea Tar Pits in Los Angeles, California, USA.

The ice and melting permafrost in Siberia have revealed ancient carcasses, too. Recent finds include woolly mammoths, cave lions, cave bears, and wolves.

giant ground sloth

Trace fossils are the other main group of fossils. Trace fossils show how an organism lived.

Footprints, or tracks, are one type of trace fossil. Tracks formed when an animal walked across soft ground, like mud. The footprints hardened and were preserved in time. A path of footprints is called a trackway.

Tracks show whether an animal walked on two feet or four. The distance between tracks can be used to calculate the animal's size and speed. Tracks might show that an animal was injured and limped. Trackways with lots of prints going the same direction are a sign that the animals traveled in herds.

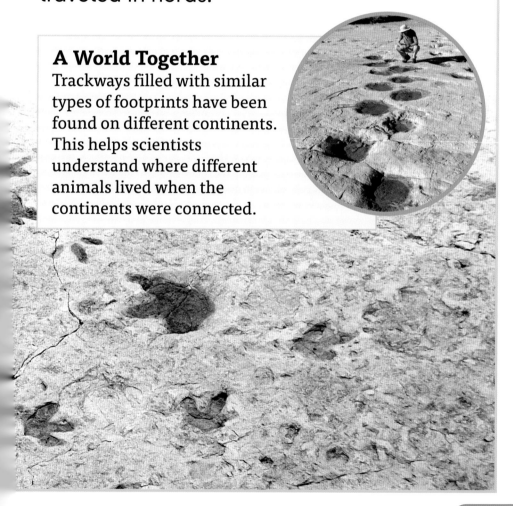

A World Together

Trackways filled with similar types of footprints have been found on different continents. This helps scientists understand where different animals lived when the continents were connected.

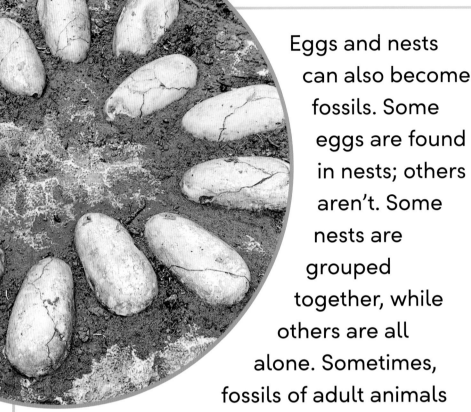

Eggs and nests can also become fossils. Some eggs are found in nests; others aren't. Some nests are grouped together, while others are all alone. Sometimes, fossils of adult animals are found nearby. These trace fossils are clues that tell us about the animals, too.

fossilized dinosaur eggs

Underground Fossils

Animal burrows are another type of trace fossil. They show how ancient animals lived and moved underground.

coprolites

Believe it or not, paleontologists also learn a lot from studying fossilized poop. Fossilized pieces of poop, called coprolites, are trace fossils. They can reveal what animals ate. Sometimes, poop has hidden treasures. Recently, scientists found a previously undiscovered species of beetle inside a coprolite. The beetle was 230 million years old!

Cool Fossil Finds

Through the years, people have made some pretty amazing fossil discoveries. Some of them have changed what we know about the history of Earth.

In the 1860s, scientists studied a fossil found in Germany. The 150-million-year-old fossil had traits of modern birds and extinct dinosaurs. They named it *Archaeopteryx*.

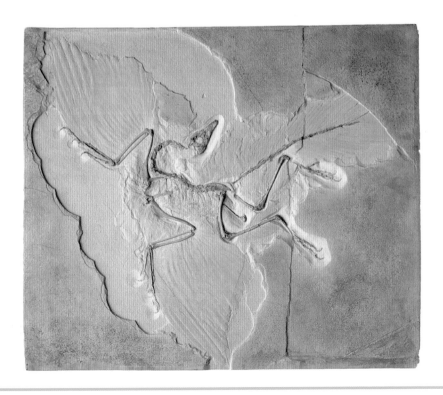

Bird, Reptile, or Both?
Archaeopteryx had a full set of teeth and a long, bony tail. Each feathered wing had three claws that could grasp prey.

When it was first discovered, some experts thought *Archaeopteryx* was the earliest bird ever found on Earth. Others thought it was the missing link between birds and dinosaurs, which were reptiles. Today, 3D scans show that *Archaeopteryx* was a dinosaur with feathers.

Some fossil discoveries add to our knowledge of a species. In 1991, researchers unearthed Scotty, a *Tyrannosaurus rex*, in Saskatchewan, Canada. Scotty was 42 feet (12.8 m) long, weighed an estimated 19,555 pounds (8,870 kg), and lived for more than 30 years. Scotty is the largest and longest-lived *T. rex* ever found.

When paleontologists examined Scotty, they found broken ribs and bite marks on his tail. These injuries show that the dinosaur fought for its long survival.

Some fossil discoveries are like taking a trip back in time. About 300 million years ago, land that is now in the central USA was closer to the equator. It was hot, wet, and covered with a tropical rainforest.

A sudden earthquake lowered the land where the rainforest stood. Soon, the rainforest was buried under mud and sand.

In 2007, geologists discovered the preserved remains of this rainforest in a coal mine in Illinois, USA. Fossils of tree trunks, leaves, fern fronds, and twigs lined the mine's ceiling. The forest is preserved forever.

Big Bugs!
Giant insects, including dragonflies as big as seagulls, lived at this time. But few animal fossils were found in the mine.

Fossils are an important tool. They are a link to the past that helps us understand the present.

Fossils tell us about extinct life. They help reveal how ancient organisms evolved into modern plants and animals. Fossils also show what the environment on Earth was like long ago. They are a record of the natural processes that have shaped Earth into the world we live in today.

petrified wood

Glossary

Amber
A hard yellow or brown fossil made from the resin of trees

Arid
Extremely dry

Body fossil
The preserved remains of dead plants or animals, such as bones, teeth, and claws

Carnivore
An animal that eats other animals

Cast fossil
A solid fossil formed when minerals fill a mold and harden in the shape of the organism

Coprolite
Fossilized poop

Excavate
To dig out and remove

Fossil
The preserved remains or traces of a plant or animal that lived long ago

Geologist
A scientist who studies Earth and how it has changed over time

Herbivore
An animal that eats only plants

Mold fossil
A fossil formed by an imprint of an organism's shape

Paleontologist
A scientist who studies plant and animal fossils to learn about the past

Petrified
Turned to stone

Preserved
Kept or saved from breaking down over time

Trace fossil
Preserved signs of an organism's activities or behavior, such as footprints or burrows

Index

Quiz

Answer the questions to see what you have learned. Check your answers in the key below.

1. What is a fossil?

2. True or False: Most of the fossils found today formed from the remains of plants and animals that lived in water.

3. What are the two main kinds of fossils?

4. True or False: Molds and casts are different types of body fossils.

5. What are three substances that have preserved the remains of entire organisms?

6. What do trace fossils show?

7. What can paleontologists learn from studying fossilized poop?

8. Which fossil helped connect modern birds and dinosaurs?

1. The preserved remains or traces of a plant or animal that lived long ago 2. True 3. Body fossils and trace fossils 4. True 5. Amber, tar, and ice 6. How an organism lived 7. What an animal ate 8. *Archaeopteryx*